In the Mind of 69

By Judith Moore

INTRODUCTION

Here are increments of thoughts from the mind of a woman age 69, randomly remembering thoughts throughout the year. There is humor, fantasy, and memories, of good and sad times. There is hope portrayed for a future for those who read this and like me they can discover their own fantasy. There are music lyrics and quotes, used for examples of the thoughts brought to a mind, when one goes off to dwell in one's own time.

I want to give full credit to the authors from the lyrics of their songs that I have chosen to refer to in my book. I am not claiming that their words are mine. I have used them because they have inspired me to think about and write about how their words have affected me. Music has always encouraged and comforted me. It has a way of describing my personality.

This is a fun book created with imagination, fiction and fantasy of what goes on in the mind of a lady experiencing life at the age of 69. You can look for humor or nonsense, fun or sadness the thoughts just travel through her mind, and she writes them down from increments of time.

I find that this is how artists become who they are. This is an inheritance or gift that God has given to each of us, whether it is a song writer, singing his /her words, or an artist drawing or painting a picture. Some may have a gift with words of poetry, or some with just a silly specialty. There are actresses, bakers, bankers, teachers, preachers, and many more. We each have our own fantasy to show.

IN THE MIND OF 69

I am a woman soon to be 69 years of age. I am willing to share with you the thoughts and desires that are flowing through the convolutions of my mind. This may seem as though I am on a fantasy trip or a trip of demented nonsense but if you wish to follow me, I will share with you increments of thought in time , from my mind , that may arise attention and stimulate you in your own time.

Today is a cool morning for the middle of April. Yesterday it actually snowed in the early morning. I am sitting in my recliner chair. It is 9:15am. I am very bored at the moment, wondering what I should do with the rest of my life. What am I doing now? My response to myself is "nothing." Perhaps, I am thinking that I would like to become a "writer." After all, we all have a story to tell; but who would be interested in reading **my** tale?

Well, I can reminisce, going back along my lifeline, it all seems so far behind. – It is over and done with. I cannot return to my past and re-do anything. I can try to hold on to memories. The good times, I will treasure, but for the most part, the time wasted with what I have done in my past is depressing. Therefore, I have allowed myself two areas in my mind to become deposit areas. One named "memory lane" and the other, my "dump bucket." Since I feel the convolutions in my mind becoming overwhelmed and uneven in weight, the bumps in my head must be growing due to the materials being collected. I am beginning to feel unbalanced with my thoughts and my words. So, I have decided to try to form another space where I can go for pleasant thoughts. This will be somewhere deep within my mind. I will call this my "happy place," and this will be where my thoughts and fantasies will be protected. In this space, the memories will be totally mine. It is here that I will allow myself to enjoy the rest of my life.

To begin with, for a brief self description of me, I now assume myself to be of average mental and health status. I was born in Winona MN. This is Polish country, although I think that I am of English, Irish, and Dutch descent. I will not claim to be German, as was my biological father. He deserted me at my age of 3 months; therefore he is buried in my "dump bucket." I am an American, and that is important to me. My mother was a good woman and taught me many valuable qualities in life. My mother is in my "happy place" and also in my "memory lane" because of her love and commitment. I grew up in a very sheltered environment. I was a nerd and a prude, in my own eyes during my young years of life. Although we lived in poverty, I had a happy childhood. The teenage years became a bit more interesting. I was a late bloomer, by my standards, marrying at age 24. I gave birth to two beautiful daughters at the age of 31 and 33. Their father is another story; as he is also in my "dump bucket," along with my biological father!

Their father divorced me when we were in our 40s. I then labeled myself as a "reject" and hit a rock on the bottom of somewhere. I may have damaged my brain cells then, for all I know, however the swelling from this experience did create and allow for more room in my brain. I became a grandmother of the best granddaughter ever, at my age of 50. From this point in time, I began a bipolar journey of travels circling around and around in the convolutions in my mind.

I have inquired friends inside my mind along the way. They occupy the space in the convolutions of my brain. They circle around the lumps and bumps and through the mountains and valleys of what I claim to be my mind, and brain space. They will make themselves known as my story continues further on.

Have you ever played "spin the bottle?" This is how my mind is traveling today. One rolls a bottle on the floor, gives it a twist with a spin, and watch where it lands. Where it lands, that is where the mind will go. I can remember, in my young years of life, this game was played a lot. I will let your imagination take you where it wants to go with that, but I will say that I have happy memories from those times.

I also spent time playing monopoly for many hours. I can remember rolling in the dough from Park Place. I also landed in jail many times. Perhaps I was a little naughty in my younger years of life.

Reminiscing a little, I recall that football was always a challenge with the boys. They liked to tackle the girls. I really had to push myself in learning how to run fast and make a quick getaway, as it seemed as though the boys liked to tackle me, leaving me to fall with bruises and skinned head.

Ice skating was always fun too, the boys liked playing "crack the whip". This is why, the boys led, leaving the girls at the tail of the line. When the boys swung around a corner, the last one of us girls went flying - that happened to be me.

The boys often gave girls rides on their bicycles. With the bike fender serving as a passenger seat, the padding did not serve too well, especially when going over bumps. I was lucky, though, when my brother gave me a ride on his bike, I was privileged to ride on his handle bars as the bike had no fender. One can imagine the comedy show we put on there.

My brother and I often played cops and robbers. He would catch me and tie me up on a chair. Then he would go out to play and I would sit all day tied up there. By now you can probably deduct that perhaps I was a little tomboy girl.

My other brother thought he was the man of the house. He often pulled my ears to make me do the dishes and work stuff. I now have big ears that buzz a lot.

My sister was gentle and kind, always coming to the rescue of the messes that I landed myself in. My mother was always working just to provide for our survival, so my sister took charge in the home as our mini-mama. Those were the days. Oh well, they are stuck in my mind. They are all in my "memory lane," as all in all that is how it began.

I have had 4 different careers in my previous adult life time. – I was a Psych Tech at a State Mental Hospital, an IBM gluer and screwer on an assembly line , a LPN at the famous Mayo Clinic, and a self employed AFCP   (Adult Foster Care Provider) for the elderly in my home which is where I am at in this point of time. This actually seems to me like a loony bin, as the elderly often become diagnosed with dementia as age sets in. Now as I am aging myself thoughts are changing. Old age is developing into retirement upon showings. I am having the silly notion of embracing these thoughts and spilling my words out in writing of this kind. With this I may have to go into hiding.

Today, thoughts are wandering through my mind. Perhaps I am searching for something left behind. The sun is shining through my window. It is a new day. I am feeling warm and happy this way. I have a lot to be thankful for. I am drinking my coffee and enjoying writing my thoughts into words. I am not hungry. I have a place to live. I have family and friends. I even have a kitty who purrs. The friends in my mind, well they are voices that keep moving around. At the moment I am at peace. I am sitting in my home with my thoughts and I am my "happy place". Whatever I am writing here, is putting me in touch with myself. It is as though I am, enclosed in stealth, traveling down a psycho path.

My thoughts are moving today with "what is it that is going help me to enjoy life?" I want to love and be loved. I want for others to love, and feel loved, I want for all people to be happy and at peace so that there is no hurt or no troubled times for anyone, anyplace. This would be the ideal, the happily ever after deal. I realize that this is an unrealistic thought for today and not possible in our worldly society this way.

The news on TV is depressing. There are terrorists in our mist. Our government is in a state of misfit. Most of our politicians seem to be corrupt and incompetent. I know that I am judgmental, due to difficult times. This is because everyone I know seems to be falling behind. There are hurricanes, floods and earthquakes here and there. There is war in Afghanistan and nuclear and mass destruction weapons hidden somewhere. Israel is bombing, and Obama is stalling. The doom and gloom that is about to come makes me wonder, Barack Husain where on earth is he from. I will drop these thought in the "dump bucket", as I am negatively judgmental and I am not a democrat. I am moving on.

Today, I am going to travel back into my memory lane and reminisce about frogs. For some reason I am finding humor in the thought of frogs. I just recently attended a conference, where the speaker talked about frogs. Frogs in kitchen, frogs in den, frogs in the court yard, frogs in the pen, frogs in the soup, and frogs could even be in the poop. Frogs everywhere, even in my mind. My analogy of the frogs is producing humor in me. I am now thinking of Bible times, when Pharaoh would not let his people go out of bondage. In a sense, I have been in bondage in my own mind from the experiences left from behind. I cannot change the past. I married the wrong man. He dumped me, he was a frog, and he jumped away. After many years, within my own mind, I have been able to put him behind. I have discovered that I can now re-live the past in my own private time. I can dump the thoughts of rejection and I can move on. I can find entertainment from the frogs jumping in my mind.

Recently, after 50 years, I was able to meet up with and again date my high school sweetheart friend. He was a tender, loving, charming young man that I dated 50 years ago back then. I have a story to tell about him but for now I'll just let myself mend. The reason being is that he is a frog man too, jumping away, and leaving me to stew. Again, he has left my world and broken my heart. Now he can just go jump in the dump bucket, as we shall part. The pains of rejection have hit me again, however, I am choosing to move on ahead and let my fantasy begin.

The sun is out today. It's a beautiful day. After months of doom and gloom with the never ending snow and rain, we are finally approaching May again. I have my windows open. The fresh air is flowing through the room as I sit in my chair pondering thoughts of what a peculiar day this is here. I am a caregiver for the elderly. I should not be revealing the activities that have gone on in this house today, because we are all considered vulnerable with hippa law in play. However, I do have to admit that I am exposing my thoughts about my activities from the day. They are that, I feel as though I have entered into a "loony bin".

My day began as I woke up from a dream that I was fishing little poops out of the toilet. I had an orange fishing pole with a red and white dare devil on it. About every ½ minute an alarm would go off, playing music to the tune of, "oh I wish I was in the land of cotton." This tune was entering my hearing canal because I do have door alarms ringing out this noise, in this house, with this tune, everywhere. The "I wish I was in the land of cotton," alerts me as to when one is entering or running away. This is a safety feature that I use because I occasionally do have demented, wandering residents. The alarm began at 5:15 am and continued on and off during the day. As the day progressed this alarm has averaged to play about every ½ hour due to 3 of the residents at play. Then, while cleaning a residents room, to my surprise I found something very unacceptable in a drinking glass, I won't go there, I'll just let that pass… Later in the day I find myself picking a resident up off the floor as the toilet seat was missed, poop was deposited, and more. On a serious note, in another room, a dear resident was unresponsive, and closing down soon. My time with her was very intense;

the timing was all within Gods suspense. I proceeded to sit myself down to take a break, only to have my kitty jump upon me and lick my face. I then am experiencing a paw on my nose, as though she is trying to hold me down or possibly wake me up to let me go. I lost track of time and was late with supper. I spilled the soup on the floor, burned the buns, and wouldn't you know onion juice went up my nose. Then the sweet little 90 year old wander woman returned home after being out on the town. She was all happy with smiles from ear to ear. Her words for me were, "I missed you honey, you are one in a million." You're an angel, you're a dear, I'm glad you're here. " The last call for the night came to me about at about 10pm, in the tune of "jingle bells, jingle bells, jingle, jingle, and jingle." This resident wanted to know what time it was and if she was dead or alive? What a day! And yes, there was a full moon in the evening sky.

I love to listen to music when times are quiet and I am feeling emotional .Country music has so many different stories to tell. I find myself going to my "happy place," as I listen to the words that others combine with the tune of music. So many times, I can relate to what they are sharing in their words of song. For example, "*She's got a Radio Heart*" - "Shine *on me Sunshine*"- "*It's a Skipity Do Da Day*," - "*Could I Have this Dance*", "*I Will Always Love You*" and "*Crazy*." - To name a few.

It is now 3:15 am. The night is very still and dark. It is very quiet in my house. I cannot seem to sleep. Thoughts are going through my mind of another frog man that I have recently stumbled on. Not only is he is a friend, but he is also a mender of the mind. How unique is that, to enjoy this type of friend. We seem to have common threads with each other with our own issues. I can sit in my recliner chair and be just me. He seems to understand, and his psychiatric fee is free.

I am restless this morning and I don't know why. It is a beautiful day outside. The sun is shining brightly and it is about 70 degrees. I am stuck in this house that I call my, loony bin box. I am tied down 24/7 to my commitment here. It really is a privilege and honor to be allowed to provide for the elderly, but I am sometimes unclear. Burn out seems to be around the bend. I am having the urge of wanting to break away. I would like to travel, but I am afraid to go alone.

If I allow myself to go in to my happy place" I can have a fantasy trip on my own. I can imagine that I am walking along a sandy beach, somewhere where the sand is almost as white as snow. The sand is soft and moist, as it is squeezing up between my toes. There is a light warm breeze, and waves of water gently pushing upon the beach. There are shells from the sea appearing everywhere that I can see. I am finding myself stooping over to pick them up. I am thinking there is a story to be told from all this stuff. I am thinking, once upon a time something lived in side this shell. As I rise up, I find myself facing a bright warm sunny, I better not tell. There seems to be an instant chemistry of energy in the mist. As I reach for a hand, I am lead on. I have no idea where I am going with this.

I love listening to music when times are quiet. Eddie Rabbit was one of the many favorite song writers that I enjoyed. He wrote "Someone Could Lose a Heart Tonight"and I Love a Rainy Niter." Then there is Annie Murrays, "Could I Have this Dance." And Dolly Pardons "I Will Always Love You." Now, I have just recently come to appreciate the rock band, Pink Floyd, as I visited the "Dark Side of the Moon," combined with the Wizard of Oz Video.

It is snowing outside today. This is almost unreal. It is May 2, 2013. We have a major snow storm in progress. 13 ½ inches + and heavy wet snow still falling. It is like winter wonderland in good ole Minnesota. The trees are beautiful and heavy laden with snow. The birds are nowhere in sight, and the tulips are covered, right? The electric power is out, so there is nothing one can do but sit and wait for the snow to pass through. This is unusual, as it is a first for history here. This is an example to us all, that God is in control. As I am drinking my cold coffee, I am reminded of how lucky I am to have what I have and do what I can.   At the moment, I am not cold, and I have shelter from the wind and snow. This is to be a lesson of some sort for me to learn, I know. The moments seem still and quiet to me, and I am very bored so I will just go to my fantasy.

Without electricity and I have no batteries, there is no way for me to turn on my radio for music, I see. At the moment, the thought of the Pink Floyd band and his music put to the video of the "Wizard of Oz"   is rolling through my mind. Pink Floyd sings about a lunatic and I am reminded of me. He sings about a lunatic on the grass, and that spoke to me. I am like a lunatic, wanting to be myself. I have my own crazy ideas of wanting to write all kinds of stuff. I am chasing this lunatic thought, throughout the curves and folds in my mind. It has landed in my thoughts and it thinks I am its home. "*The Dark Side of the Moon*," is the name of Pink Floyd's album. My ideas of my life can relate to what I have seen and heard from this scenario. Judy Garland plays the actress role in the Wizard of Oz. She is a fun loving child playing on a fence. She falls off but is not hurt. Then someone takes her dog away (her best friend) and she is traumatized. A tornado storm comes up and every one runs for shelter. She is left to fend for herself. She bumps her head and goes off into a fantasy. She is just like me. - My name is also Judy, although there is no "garland" in me. *"Who really knows who I am, and who is who, and what lies around the bend for me or for you?   Round and round and round I go, I have found how to live without, and I have found what life is all about. Follow me in my fantasy. Who cares if the lunatic is on the grass, I am insane, roll me up and lock the door."* – *"Time by Pink Floyd,"* is in my head, I am swirling around and around and more. Soon I will be on the floor. - make fun of me, I will find my own friends in my own fantasy. *"I can touch, taste, and see. I can like or I can hate, - How I live my life will be my life and when the work is done, I can close down and get another one."*

      I have learned to appreciate Pink Floyd's music, because of these words that he sings and how they are brought out in his music. His words and music can take me off into LaLa fantasy land in my own imagination and time. I have arrived in my "happy place" today.

      From my observation of the " Wizard of Oz" video and Pink Floyd's music, Judy Garland meets up with her friends, the scarecrow, tin man and lion and they become partners on their journey. In her Oz land, they all have their troubles and problems that need fixing. They all have dreams of hope and happiness. They can run, hide, hurt, hunt, and even cry. They are taken away by the moment that leads into darkness and hard times. They are racing around only to find out that the sun is the same, the witch is at play and flying away, and the scarecrow is coming undone. The lion is fighting and the dog is on the run.   Then one day only to find that ten years have gone by, they are one day closer to death and they are losing their time. The castle door is closing, they surrender, and they give up. Their money they hide, they run, they get away, and then they say keep your hands off my stuff. What is there to choose to do? They can face the devil, smoke, burn, run or turn back, but in the end they go round and round", like in a hamster trap. *"It can't be helped. Time is running out.   Know that you can choose to love, you can choose to hate, you can choose to care, or you can choose to create.   Do all you can do to make it through? Don't be afraid to care, and don't be afraid to leave. Run until the work is done. Time is running out.   Remember those who gave you a chance, the lunatic is there from the past."* This is all in my head, you can lock me up and you can throw me away, I'll just go home and jump into my fantasy. In my imagination, in the convolutions of my mind, I have made this journey many times.

The snow is subsiding tonight. Darkness is setting in. Tomorrow is another day soon to begin again. It is now 3 Am. I am awakened to a snow plow rumbling by outside. It is snowing again .The doorbell goes off-"*Oh I wish I was in the land of cotton*." The little wander woman is trying to open the door. "I need fresh air," she says, as a snow drift blows in and falls onto the floor. The "lunatic" inside of me is saying "what is this on my floor that I see?" I want to go back to bed, but there is the sound of another stumbling around. I'm afraid soon he will be falling behind. I need to go back to sleep to finish my dream. I was in my "happy place" there, and now the thought is gone. I turn the TV on and I see, someone trying to sell knives to me. I change the channel, and the monsters are cheating on their wives. I remember the thought, - "*Life is short, ten years can pass and you can't go back.*" The morning network news just coming on and is telling of how 3 girls have escaped from years of being held in captive by a mental loony man. How awful it is that! Evil does exist. My prayer is that there could be a little more love in the world of "IS." I heard a song that Annie Murray sang yesterday, it was about "*A little Good News today.*"

It is soon to be the "*Ides of June*". Tomorrow I will be turning the time. So now my thoughts will be "In the Mind of 69." I have been warned about using this phrase as a title. Only those who wish to misunderstand it could possibly be a little dysfunctional. As for me, I can honestly admit that I will be 69, and that I am a little bit crazy and a little behind. At my age, my convoluted brain cells are like well aged, good tasting wine. My values have changed over these past years. I have experienced many changes, and have had many tears. I am no longer the "poor me, life has not been fair" person held dear. I am no longer the serious, wannabe, proper, polite, caregiving person that I have hopefully portrayed here. For many past years, I have devoted my service towards helping others, now I want to give to my children and who knows the others. I am now sharing my thoughts with those of you that might want to see the other side of me, or perhaps you will see that you too could have a lunatic inside of you, just like me.

Tomorrow I will be traveling to Sioux City to attend a Rick Springfield Concert. This will be held in the midst of a motorcycle rally. Who knows, maybe I will decide to ride off into the yonder on the back of a motorcycle, hanging on to a greasy pony tail. I will carry a little spray can of mace in my pocket, just in case I need it. But then on the other hand, I might meet up with a premium Harley Davidson hunk frog man, and who knows what might happen to me when I land. I will listen to Rick as he sings "Jesses Girl". I will be in my "fantasy land", in my own little world. I will take him into my dreams and wheee, I will wonder, "is this really me." All of this, whatever happens, I will plant in my fantasy.

Today is now June 14. I am on my way for a new adventure. My daughter is taking me to the Bikers Rally in Sioux City Iowa. First we attended a funeral of a co worker, who was also a biker. There were long haired grease looking bikers, frogs, musicians and friends all amongst them. As we left the scene, the music from Norman Greenbaum was playing "Spirit in the Sky." It was as though we were being sent off on a mission to fly. A voice inside of me was telling, we are not to judge and we are to just enjoy what we see.

After arriving at the hotel, we shuttled over to the Rally grounds. We mingled a bit, observing the crowd. We then stumbled on to Santa Klaus .He was a very congenial biker man, and he allowed me a seat on his motor cycle. I felt like Miss Queen Bee at the time. I looked for a pony tail, but he had none. He was a very clean cut, polite, biker man. So I did not ride off into the yonder like my fantasy had planned. I played it safe with just a pose a long. Later in the evening we went over to the music grounds, and landed up dead center front in the mash pit pile. The rock band Saliva was performing. The music was an awakening. It was as though I was entering another world of fantasy. There was a tornado watch out, and the sky became yellow. One could not tell if it was a train roaring through or the band playing heavy metal. The security guards were busy breaking up fights. One man was being lifted and passed through the crowd as though he was on a flat slab created for the dead. I then got kicked in the head. A very kind, clean cut biker man, Scott, took to protecting me and to my surprise, - I was in wonderment, was he hitting on me? He was only 50 and me; you see 69, tee hee. Could I possibly be a "cougar" by him flattering me? His eyes were as blue as the sky, and well me, I was having thoughts about entering a frog fantasy.

June 15, my birthday has arrived. I am spending the whole afternoon sitting in a mash pit spot waiting for Rick Springfield to arrive. Kory and the Blowfish arrived before Rick, singing the song "It will be alright." Candlestick, another band that played, passed their rock music through my ears as they banged away in my head. I was beginning to wonder, am I going to be alright? The final moment came when Rick Springfield arrived, awesome as usual, winking his eye. He began singing "Jesses Girl," then "Beautiful me." He melted my heart and he reassured me as he sang his song, "Don't talk to Strangers," while biker Scott was smiling at me. A frog was jumping inside my mind could this have been another frog man moment at that time? Unfortunately the weekend passed and reality hit. I had to return home. The experience from this journey will go into my "memory lane" pit.

This weekend, I am again bored with my limited entertainment of watching TV. The only news worthy event available to me was the performance of the Great Walando walking his tight rope over the Grand Canyon, whoopee. Who in their right mind would want to challenge fate like that? He did succeed, proving that dreams can come true. For me, the lunatic in my mind   will not even challenge the imagination of walking on a rope of this kind. The lunatic plans to stick in the grass and I will keep eccentric dreams like this in my fantasy past.

It is raining again today. It has rained in increments daily if not nightly for the past three months. The corn will not be knee high by the fourth of July. It is mostly not even planted. We are becoming like a rain forest in Minnesota. The trees are in full bloom and the grass is almost knee high. The lunatic in me is lying in the grass. It could be stuck in the mud, but instead its thoughts are rolling through my head. I have to wonder if I should begin building an Ark. The dark side of the moon seems to be rising. The IRS is stealing my money, and our country is going broke. This is not funny. The baby boomers are getting old, Medicare is changing and Obama care will soon be No care for the aged. The kids will be paying our debts through their nose. In my mind, I will soon have to get out the water hose. I will be changing course with these words of thought; I will flush them away with water into the sewage pot.

My "happy place "is right around the bend. I am now finding myself on the mend. I have acquired an old, new, beautiful white friend. Jimmy is its name, it has bucket seats, with 4 wheel drive, and it is all customized. This will take me places that I have not been.

Well today is another day. I am thinking about what is happening in my Loony Bin Box, what I can say. My imagination is taking me away. Off I go into my fantasy of a dark side of the moon mood, as I entertain thoughts of this loony bin guru. I began hearing, "You ugly old hag! Where did you come from? You old hen? It's you again, you old grizzly. The river it is red and slimy and I am going to dump you upside down in it. Get out of here you old hen. "

As I am walking down the hallway of this highly respected dementia center, I am asking myself, "what am I doing, am I going to be here forever?" The year seems to be passing by and like ten years, I still cannot fly.

The sunlight is penetrating brightly thru the window now and there is a feeling of warmth surrounding me somewhere. As I look to the outside, I am observing the lunatic laying in the grass. It is looking at me. "What is it doing there?" I ask. Moving forward, I slipped and almost took a tumble as I hydroplaned across the floor on a huge puddle .This is what happens when I don't pay attention . "Where did that puddle come from?" I am wondering. I turned my head around only to see, the vision of a dirty old man trying to pee on me. "Morbidly stupid and very Gross," were the words from my mind, as I passed by the kitchen area in this loony bin. I happened to notice a cook dressed in white, with a red bandana tied over his nose tight. His chef hat was standing stately straight up and his pants were low, by his knees as he held them tight. The crack of his butt was peering above, there was a strong aroma odor and it looked like fudge. It smelled like cooked cabbage and boiled egg farts, as the smell morbidly dissipated out. There was no doubt in my mind where this odor came from. I quickly left the scene, as I became faint and numb. Affixation was waiting at my entry gate. The emesis inside my intestine began to stir, and before I could stop, the upchuck clumps of cheese and brown curds came up. I tried to contain the remains in my hands, but to no avail, they slipped through my fingers and into a pan. I was unaware, that the demented lady had also been following me. She then slipped over the pan and fell into the pee... I had no remorse for her and that scene, so off I went into more fantasy. I headed for the wash room looking for a place to lie down. Then I remembered, the lunatic, it was on the ground. Should I go there or should I pass? My imagination was sliding through the grass. I must abort these thoughts from my mind. Writing a book of this sort will not create any good thoughts. I'll send this story   into   the "dump bucket" in my mind.

Thursday is the 4th of July. Everyone seems to have plans but me. Once again my fantasy will set me free. I will honor our freedom and go into my "happy place." Wander woman has entered my head. "You're one in a million," she said. "You're an angel; you're a sweetheart, now you get a good rest. What would I do without you, you are the best." On my way looking for a restful place, Hoobstank was playing over the radio waves. I reminded myself that like in this music ,I do need a good rest. As I listen to the lyrics of reason from Hoobstank, - *"I'm not a perfect person, there are many things I wished I didn't do, but I continue learning and so I just have to say this to you. Before I go, I want you to know, that I found a reason for me, to change who I use to be, a reason to start over new, I found a reason to show, a side of me you didn't know."* - This master piece of music is floating through my head into the core of my soul. I am free to be me, and I am enjoying my fantasy.

Today is a new day. All is quiet and well in the house. I am sitting in my recliner with my feet up.

Thoughts are wandering through my mind. Last night the "mind mender frog friend" visited me. We enjoyed each other's company. It is so nice to have a common thread that seems to run through both of our heads. I am a serious sort of person, just trying to get in touch. I am looking for that "happy place," I am not looking for much. I am in need of a friend who just accepts and understands, this is me, and I am who I am, and I am just me. I know that I can shut down and I can begin again, or I can decide to fly away until the end.

On the serious side of life, and after a recent visit with a doctor, I have been diagnosed with warts behind my ear. Now who and how does one get warts there? A lump, hiding back and behind my ear is like finding another lunatic peer. It has gone unnoticed, until the crud build up began to itch. Now in my thoughts, I am thinking the lunatic in my mind has found a ditch. The lunatic thinks that it can live in me, and it has hooked tight like a hitch you see. I must abort this thought and move on. Dump bucket in the loony bin, here it comes.

I went to a casino today. I blew my money away. It could have been just another day, a day of wasting my life away. One could say that I am bored. I need some excitement in my life, to look forward for. I can go into my fantasy and search for someone, but in the reality I find none. My self confidence is low so who would want to know me. I guess these thoughts should head over and out from my fantasy.

It is raining this morning. It is dark, humid and gloomy outside. The sun is supposed to come out, but it has not yet made an appearance. I am confined in my loony bin box, sitting in my recliner chair with my feet up and my kitty at my side. My kitty is like a little angel sent from above. My kitty unconditionally loves me. All she seems to want from life love. Pets are really awesome. They know how one feels before we know ourselves, and my kitty comforts me. She can sense a lunatic in the grass, or the Spirit in the mass. My kitty likes to eat cheese. She likes to hide in boxes and drawers; she scales the walls and scratches the floors. She jumps and flies across the room, she likes to play with balls and brooms. Like the lunatic she is free to pounce, and like the Spirit, she is in my house. My kitty is like an angel to me.

After watching the movie "Notting Hill" with Julia Roberts and Hugh Grant, on TV, I am sent off into my fantasy world again today. Julia is so beautiful, with her smile and awesome acting ability. To me she is the most beautiful woman in the world. And Hugh, he is definitely a "10". Although he is portrayed as such an innocent gentle man. My thoughts are "oh if I could only be as beautiful as Julia" and "if only there was a handsome gentle man like Hugh pursuing and wanting me." but In reality there is none, I have never known or felt this experience, you see. I am just plain Judy. I am just me. However, in my fantasy, I will go into my dream land mode. Here, I can find my own love I'm told.

In my mind from memories of my high school years, the sweetheart frog friend comes back into view. Now, out of sight and out of mind, somewhere he is still lingering on. I know that he is not available for me. He has dumped, jumped and set himself free. Like the lunatic laying in the grass - I can close this journey down, I can shut the door and I can start all over again. After all, I tell myself there are frogs in the forest and frogs in the pond, what makes me think they're not all around?

As I continue on in my fantasy trail, I can stumbled upon a handsome, ordinary , common, intelligent frog man somewhere. His eyes will be blue, and he will be 6 foot 2. His physique will be like Hugh, and he will say, "I want you." As he moves closer to me with a smile and a kiss. I now do not know what to do with this. My heart is melting and I am in awe with the thought that this handsome frog man would want me at all. He tells me nice words, and appreciates me. We both will enjoy each other's company.

Another day is passing by. It is "Manic Monday" all the way. Things get a little hectic in my loony bin box on this day, I know, there are many bills to pay. My bank account is running low so, it is back to work again I go. I now find myself accidentally falling off into a fantasy show. The lunatic is in the grass in my mind. My earth has rolled over and I have fallen into the sea. I am looking up and the dark side of the moon is facing me. In reality, I am 69, and now I must learn that I need to let go of the time that is not mine. I am no longer the chick that I used to be, I am an old hen stuck in my loony bin, as you can see. Tonight I was choked by this demented resident. "I was only trying to help," I said. I feel no appreciation for what I do, so why should I care - oh pooh. My caregiving career is about to end as I no longer have it in me again. I am burning out and giving up, all I should do now is lie down in the grass and pout. Life does goes on day after day, but "what is the use?" I find myself say. What I have spent a life time learning has only turned into everyday enduring. The young ones have the answers and techniques, what have I accomplished, where is my boutique? My children would be better off if I were dead. I have life insurance on my head. I am ready to give up and let it all pass, what is the use – the lunatic is in the grass. I must close this thought, and pitch it in the dumb bucket. This thought is useless I should just plucket.

I am sitting here tonight with my daughter as she is studying for a chemistry exam. She is studying for her PHD and wants to find the cure for the loony demented people like me. I am wondering if osmosis is setting in. There are alkaloids and pheldamehide, analtoids and odd shaped halogoids, all unfamiliar to me. There are molecule penphoids, moles, and hydroidides, who knows these three? Butane is the condensed structure with chh-ding doing dee, whee, the lunatic is in the grass laughing at me... My daughter knows how to draw the skeletal structure of a butane alkine wine bound structure, now I wonder is she going to make a bomb constructure. This is getting a little taxing on my brain I think that I have lost my mind. After all, I am 69 and a little behind; I just need to jump off this runaway train.

Today I will write about the motives in my mind. The lunatic is not lying in the grass. The lunatic is roaming about in the convolutions of my brain mass. Around and around up and down through the mountains, valleys and beyond in my brain. I am beginning to feel weak. I am asking myself again, "I wonder what lies around the bend? So, ok, today I am 69 - the "golden years" will soon be behind. I wonder, "What does this mean?" As I see what has happen with my residents, I really do not want this to happen to me. I do not want to be demented in anger and hate, or lose my mind to time and place. I do not want my limbs to wiggle and collapse, I do not want to shake or become over baked, I do not want to be stinky or whatever this makes. The thought of pain with an incurable disease only begins to frighten me. In reality I am in this Loony Bin, and I am a sacrifice of caregiving for these friends. I am trying to do what is right and expected of me but in my mind there may be a motive with a fee. How will I survive this until eternity? I have bills to pay, so I am not free. My thoughts are depleting, and fear is inside of me, what if I become loonier than what I can see.

Today is very hot outside. The thermometer is reading 93. I am sitting in my recliner chair with my feet up. I am free. Once again doing nothing but passing music through my ears .Because I am feeling a little out of sorts, I am listening to the music "Unwell" by Matchbox. I can relate so very much to some of their words of song. - *"All day staring at the ceiling making friends with the shadows on my wall, - All night hearing voices telling me get some sleep,   tomorrow might be good for something - Hold on, - I'm feeling like a breakdown - Well, I'm not crazy - I'm just a little unwell - I know right now you cannot tell - but stay a while and then you will see - a different side of me   - I know you don't care - but soon enough you're going to think of me as how I used to be - pretty soon they will come to get me ."* No need to take me away, the Loony Bin is here. Here I am, and I'm on the way. Tee hee, my sweet fantasy.

I spent an awesome yesterday rolling up and down the river on a Sunday afternoon with my daughter and son-in law. The boat ride was   exciting and eventful. I was the polka queen dancing in the open bow of their Tahoe Impulse boat. The bald eagles were flying overhead and there was a bald headed man sitting on a cruise liner in a lock and dam, hanging on a rope with one hand. I thought that he was waving to me, but unfortunately it was the movement of the water, as we were being raised and levitated up higher. We passed by a nuclear power plant and several trillion dollar mansions, as they stood stately high upon the bluffs. It was as though we owned the river. We were feeling free as the breeze. The music by Pink Floyd was playing, and   "Shine on Crazy Diamond" was flowing. - "Remember when you were young, you shone like the sun. Now the look in your eyes they are like black holes in the sky. You reached for the secret to soon, you cried for the moon. Now you are riding in the breeze, nobody knows how near you are." I am thinking, "I don't want to get old; I don't want to be 69. I don't want to die. I just want to be young.   I want to bask in the shadow of yesterday. I want to be young again, this year. I want to sail on in the breeze; I want to float in the sun. I want to shine with my kids, I want to shine on. "

We stopped on the beach and squeezed our toes through the sand, and then we moved on towards the setting sun. We approached the "Jamaican Hut" and ported there. I was teased by a brain freeze, and now my mind went somewhere. After this day was done, I had to return home. All I can say is "thank you" my sweet kids Sara and Shaun, I love you so, I had enormous fun. Into my "Memory lane", this I flung.

Now, I have dreams in my fantasy of owning a houseboat. I will float down the river and learn to hold on. I will stop by all the sand bars and enjoy the serenity of the peace and the light from the sun. The stars can come out freely into the night and UFOs can even fly by like shooting stars if they like. I will gaze at them in awe, wondering who they are. Could they be our departed loved ones from above or perhaps more frog men from the planet Mars. The water will be soothing as a warm breeze passes by. I will bask in the sun as I close my eyes. The sand will coat my feet, and I will forget to eat. I will sleep rolling through the waves and I will awake with no pressure to have to please. My life will be at total ease. Fish and turtles will swim on by, and there might even be some frogs jumping around. I will not be alone, as in my fantasy I can create a clone. This thought will have to find its way to my "fantasy" as in reality I must return home.

My mind is caught up in tangles tonight. The lunatic is on the loose running through the convolutions of my mind. I am full of confusion and grief. It is the human condition that is holding me tight. Everything seems to be centered on energy I've learned. The cosmic approach as one connects with another is an unexplainable concern. A quote from an unknown origin, "What you see in another is a reflection of what dwells from within." is caught up in my mind, and I need to put it behind. I have just had the most frustrating confrontation with a demented resident again. There is anger and aggressive behavior coming towards me. I have to wonder what I have done to deserve this. I am not free. I feel offended and abused, - poor me. - If what I see in another is a reflection of what dwells from within, then I am befuddled unexplainably. The lunatic is telling me, I'm silly and abnormal. I need to let go of this idea, shut the door, and think of this no more. So, ok, I do not feel as though I am angry, I have to let go. I must abandon this malady. I can I go into my fantasy. It is here I will find, like in the Pink Floyd Wizard of Oz scenario, "my life is my life and if I don't like the way it is, I can shut the door and get a new one." I must not take offense. The Spirit is inside of me, it has come to my rescue and it is telling me "forgive and set yourself free."

Ok, so now today I am confronted with I am not crazy, - I am just a little abnormal. I am bothered with buzzing in my ears, it's horrible. The sound is like a tea pot full of steam ready to explode. I have discovered that the "Dump Bucket"deposit areas in my mind are near my ears and behind my nose. The circulations of events are piling up. I must be overloaded with thoughts tangled up creating this pressure that is ready to blow. This is like a phantom putting on a show. I must look for another route and learn to let go. This buzzing in my ears is an irritating overload.

My friend, Bonnie, just passed away today. It happened on her birthday. Lewy bodies took over her brain cells. Now what was fair about that? In my thoughts, I want to think that the lunatic in her mind threw her in a crack with no way back. Our minds should know when there is danger prowling and lurking around. Those lewy bodies need to be sent away. To the "dump bucket "I say. However in reality we have no choice with our flesh condition. God is the one in control of our condition. Bonnie had no choice in this matter, I know. Her time was up. 10 years have passed by, and now she is gone. At Bonnie's funeral my brain waves floated towards my "memory lane" as I thought of all the fun times we had through the years. Bonnie was an avid and most beautiful dancer. She glided and waltzed around the dance floor with her dear, sweet Willard. We had parties, and fun and even a few bottles of wine .We knew how to laugh and we knew how to dine.

Now at my age of 69, it is brought into my view that life can be short, and end abruptly in a moment of time. Bonnie made it thru 79- just 10 years more and this scene could be mine.   Bonnie's words for me, - "When you come to the end of the day, and the sun has gone away, don't linger in a gloom, let your soul bloom. Miss me a little, but let me go, for this is a journey we all must know. When you are lonely and sick at heart, go to a friend you know, bury your sorrow in doing well - miss me a little, but let me go."

I'm feeling a little emotional and overwhelmed with the thoughts that are flowing through my mind today. Bonnie has passed and two more have followed that way.   Death seems to be on the door step today. I am just going to enter into my world of fantasy and dwell on some words of music from some of the favorite song artists to me. Christy Lanes, *"I Had a Dream"* her words - *" if you see the wonders of all the fairy tales , you can take the future, even if you fail - I believe in angels - something good in everything I see, - I believe in angels when I know the time is right for me."*   and Annie Murrays - *"You Needed Me, - "I cried a tear, you wiped it dry, - I was confused, you cleared my mind, - I sold my soul, you brought it back to me, - you held me up and gave me dignity ,"* and don't forget Whitney Houston's ' - *"Greatest Love of All" - "I believe the children are the future, teach them well and let them lead the way, show them all the beauty they possess inside, give them a sense of pride to make it easier, let the children's' laughter remind us how we used to be, learning to love yourself is the greatest love of all. My thoughts with this are that "God is the greatest love of all, and His Spirit is inside you and me."*

I love my children, my daughters, I have three. Actually I have two daughters, one granddaughter, and possibly I could claim an adoptee, Doreen. They are my children, they a part of me. What I want most of all is for them to be healthy, happy and free. My prayer is that their dreams will come true. Anything is possible, believe, that's all we have to do. Trust and obey is the only way. Dreams can come true every day. The love that we will feel is the love that dwells inside of us, you and me.

I took a drive with my Jimmy today. I just had the feeling of running away. I drove 40 miles north, with no sense of destination in sight. I passed a sign for a demolition, what a fright. 3 deer crossed my path and some wild turkeys took flight. The lunatic woke up and tried to get me up tight, so   I made u turn and returned home, right.

I' m still 69 and I am looking behind, Many years have passed by and now I must to decide, -what do I do now? How do I get there from here?

I m so tired of this loony bin, that I am stuck in here. A demented resident is getting me down. There is no appreciation for what I do, so I think in my mind, "what is the use."I am punched and hit in the boob, choked and hair pulled too. I ask again, "what is the use?" I have no recourse, I am in disarray. The Spirit says "just let it goes, just forgive, look the other way." But like the lunatic has told me before, I can just shut down. I can just shut the door. This is a scary thought be fronting me, I could sell my house and then what if it don't work out ? The Spirit tells me, there can be a new beginning.

Today, my mind is befuddled. The lunatic is stuck. My thoughts are racing around in confusion and   my mind is full of muck.   There is no filter as to where my thoughts are going. There is no direction, and my thoughts are rolling. I am getting tired and depressed and I have no hope for rest. My vocation of helping the elderly is not really the best. The demented lady is again wearing me down. I am tired of getting my hair pulled and boobs pushed around. Thoughts of retirement are weighing me heavily down. After all I am 69. The lunatic is telling me – "shut the door, you can shut down." If there is nothing left, 10 years can pass by, then it can be gone. The voice of the Spirit arrives on the scene; it says, "perk up, my child, get yourself busy and look for faith, hope and charity."

I went on road trip to clear my mind and to get myself back on track from this human life time. My daughter took me for a drive to Winona. I was again on the loose and out of my box arena. On the way we stopped in Chatfield, and there we abducted Doreen. Laughter medicine entered our minds as we headed south and around the bend. She was obsessed with finding air time on her phone. Her conversations with the operator were, " I worked all night, I need a shower, I just want some air power, I've been kidnapped and I don't know where I am , just give me some air – some air time now . Air, can you speak English, air, I already paid, I just want some freaking air. Can't you care"! During that time a huge burp belch came from the driver, and laughter erupted like almost forever. As we rolled through the country side, we stopped at a little store in the middle of nowhere. It was built in the 1870s, had a wood floor and lots of old relics and more. A little ole lady was sitting   in a chair. She said "just pay for your stuff over there". She directed me behind the counter and had me open the cash drawer. She said, "it's on your honor. You need to put your money in there." I began to sense the lunatic in my mind prowling, the Spirit was prodding me, and I was shaking. As we ventured on our way, the beauty of the hills, trees and valleys were a fabulous give away.

We were headed for "God's Country" abounding. Memories were taking me back to my beginnings. The valleys and the bluffs were reminding me of my childhood years. I was born in Winona, surrounded by beautiful hills and bluffs, the Mississippi River and all good stuff. We moved to Lamoille, when I was young, which was a tiny little river town. The beauty of God's creation was all around .As kids we played on the home made fishing rafts and we had lots of fun. We ran through the meadows, as the snakes layed low in the field basking in sun. At age 6, I was hit by a car that did not yield , my head suffered an injury and now my mind is a little unclear. However I survived that scene and I have moved on.

Now, Back in Winona, we enjoyed a nice lunch and then drove up on the Garvin Heights hill, which will give anyone an enormous thrill. Standing stately high upon the bluff, we were overlooking the whole city of Winona, and all the river stuff. Sugar Loaf, Lake Winona, the Mississippi River   barges, and islands, the trees gave way to the country side marvels. Time was passing and before we knew, we were on our way heading home, back to the Loony Bin composite . Laughter and fun had been filling our souls, but on the way home, the devil had his goal. Out in the country in the middle of nowhere, a cop came along and well speeding ticket, oh no, we met an old crow. Well, back in my box, I am here again, I'll write my stories and remember when. Thanks to my daughter, I am sane again. This I will store in my "memory lane."

Labor Day is upon us again. I have made it through 69 of them. The weather is hot and the trees are still green, school resumes, and we are still free. There is trouble on the world front today. Syria has a crisis with destruction and nerve gasses are spilled on their masses. In our own country, the blacks are killing the whites, an unexpected blow to the back, in retaliation of racial fights. The Muslims are planning a march on 9/11 in front of the White House, at seven. It was only a few years ago, our twin towers were attacked and now there are terrorist in our mist. Love and hate are like ying and yang. We are being threatened by the alkita gang. Our economy has gone down the tubes, jobs are hard to find and there's not much good news. Whatever happened to hope and change? Obama's transparency is down the drain.

Do you ever wonder about the voices inside your head? Everyone has them. Only the gifted will understand. The lunatic is again prowling around. It is in my head and it is not on the ground. We are all free to believe, and I believe, there is a Spirit inside of me. The Spirit is telling me "just forget it, you are free." I am not crazy, or abnormal you see, I might be a little impaired, but soon you will see there is another side of me. I do have that someone, very special inside . I have learned to be still, and to know that the Spirit is He! I have just discovered that the lunatic and Spirit are on a Bipolar battlefield inside of me.

My granddaughter Anna is on my mind today. I am so very proud of her in so many ways. She is beautiful and smart and she does really have a tender heart. She could easily be a movie star, a computer guru or an entrepreneur. It is amazing the creations she is able to do, it is just that she has so many things to get through. Times are tough for the young ones today. Money and jobs have gone away. Times are tough, what can I say. If I had a magic wand I would mend everything in her world today.

Since I am 69 and aging, this so fits my criteria. - I cannot see, I cannot pee, I cannot chew, and I cannot screw. I wonder what I can do? My memory shrinks, my hearing stinks, I think I smell, I look like hell. My mood is bad,- can you tell? My body is drooping, I have trouble pooping. The Golden Years have come at last. 69 will soon be in my past. My thoughts are, " it is sad, what the elderly have to look forward to, I am in hopes that I can make it through. I'm headed for the finish line, and I don't want to be left behind." I'll just dump this thought today.

I find myself thinking about the Constitution today. We are all supposed to all be created equal. We are supposed to free. One has to wonder today, what is really equal and what is free for me? We are supposed to be able to have freedom of speech. - We the people -. Who are we? The government seems to be controlling me. There is still slavery, I am 69, and I am still working full time. The taxes I have to pay – what can I say. Inflation takes a toll on the groceries anyway. My electric bill runs high both night and day, for a gallon of gas, we really pay. God has been taken out of the schools today. It's no wonder our kids are going astray. Off to the "dump bucket," for this I say.

I escaped from my loony bin today. In reality, I traveled north to the Renaissance Festival. There, I entered into another fantasy world. I was walking on wood chips and dirt, there was a haze in the air, and there was mold everywhere. I really didn't know if I was here or there. In my mind, I was not clear, I was asking myself, " was I dead or alive ?" It was with this though I went backward in time, as I passed by the queen and pirates dressed in old attire. There were robin hoods and cave men, elephants and turtles. There was mead to drink and it made me think. I observed a wooden coffin being pulled around in the dirt. I wondered if the body inside was dead or just hurt. There was a tight rope walker standing on a ladder, on a rope that was on fire as he juggled some wires. There were naughty men with potatoes in their pants, making jokes and airing their cracks. Some women were wearing corsets and showing their cups, "cup cakes, for sale, they were calling out." Some men were swinging their swords as though they were lords. At my age of 69, I rode an elephant .My butt got stretched and now it is sore. All in all it was a fun day. Home again, home again, gighety gigh. What should I say, I'll roll this into my "memory lane "and continue on the way.

Another disaster hit the news today. 12 bodies were shot away. A lone gun man, and black at that, broke into the naval yard base and shot people flat. Who knows the reason, was it disgruntled or race, or was it a terrorist or Obama issues misplaced? Our country is in such a mess. The President is avoiding the problems today. There is talk of our government shutting down . Dump the clowns in the bucket, and move on.

Passing through my mind today, I find myself wandering through the convolution that is holding the core of my being together. I am having thoughts of what am I hearing. The lunatic is lying in the grass, and I am beginning to see, the other side the Spirit real fast. It is telling me, I am free. I am free to believe and hope for the future of what I to see. I don't really have to have a fantasy, because I can see my life will be what it is meant to be. The song that is now playing through the channel of my mind is, "It is no secret what God can do. What he has done for others, He can do for you."

This morning I woke up from a confusing dream. The lunatic must have been at play or else my thoughts have just wandered away. My thoughts have been swirling around and around from one thought to another with no answer to be found .It is as though I have slid down into a deep valley, all muddled in despair. I for sure needed to find my way out of there. In my mind, I was among a group of people. I was not chosen, I was frozen. I was being pulled down with weights of some sort, and blood was in the midst, gushing from my heart. I was told to offer it up. I replied, " Is this my blood, am I dead or alive? " Then I woke up. It came into to my mind, "be still and know that - I AM." So I lay quietly, and listen and wait, my thoughts begin to hesitate. Then my thoughts, wandered all over the place. There was a vision of a burning fire. In a moment of time,in my mind, something was pushing through from behind. Could it have been that I was letting go, passing on through something, and what it was, I don't know.

It is now October 3rd. Shots are being heard outside of the capitol of Washington DC. Our government is on lock down because no one can agree. Obama Care is being forced upon everyone, you see. Our country is going is broke, and imagine, soon we will not be free. I think that anxiety is coming upon me. The "dump bucket" site is the place for this to be, because one seems to be helpless in this time of history.

Today I am having day dreams about night dreams in the middle of the afternoon. Thoughts of a Ronnie Millsap's song are flowing through my head. I am headed for my fantasy land again. I am thinking about what it would have been like to have had a soul mate. I feel as though this experience has never happened to me. It seems to be an analytical comparison as to Ronnies existence of being blind. How can one miss, what one has never had or could not see? However, I do wonder if I have missed the boat here. I feel as though I am traveling down the river looking about. I find myself asking, "Am I looking for love in all the wrong places or do I not see?" The inner Spirit voice is inside of me saying that I have to learn to love myself then I will know what love is all about.

It's raining out again. It is a cool damp October night. Our government is on the 13th day of shutdown. I am so irritated with the news on TV about the President's threats and our countries debt. All he wants to do is spend more of the people's money with no regret.

Obama care is being forced upon us. How does he expect to pay for this? Obama is driving our national debt up, it makes no sense, and our freedom is on interrupt.

I am reminded of a song sung by Bobby Goldsboro, as it flows through my mind today. I have my own version of his song, it goes this is*way* – *"In the spring of my life, you came to me , in summer you blessed me with a child, then in the fall you went away and all is gone."* After allowing these thoughts to flow through my mind, I am left with feelings of being left alone. Then another of his song lyrics came ringing through. In this I found my Spirit too. - *"And I love you so , people ask me how, how have I lived till now - I tell them I don't know. But life began again, the day you took my hand. The book of life is brief, and once the page is read, all but love is dead."*

I am getting emotional again. I have been on this battle field in my mind. The Spirit and the lunatic have been playing bipolar with me. My thoughts are rolling around and around in the convoluted folds. When it come to the Ys, and the bends, it is a guess which way it will end. When I don't always make the right choice between good or bad, I don't want to be sad. I want to be glad.

After watching the movie "*Splendor in the Grass*" more thoughts enter into my mind. Young love seems so very far behind. There is a little pouched place in the convoluted folds of my mind where those memories will just not dissipate. The image of my little frog man keeps jumping around; I wonder who he is courting at this time. Memories of a childhood song that we sang in school 60 years ago come to view - *"A frog went a courting yes he did uhum uhum, sword and pistol by his side uhum uhum , the frog said, to miss mousy will you marry me, sword and pistol by my knee, uhum uhum."* (My memory of this song is muddled and lost .) The end thought of all of this is that I am the one in this mist of these memories. My mind of 69 has rolled into another abyss.

Some days, I have no words or thoughts to share. It is as though my mind dead. I exist like a robot, wandering around instead. It is amazing how my mind can tell my body parts where to go and what to do, things that I am not even aware of too. Like every breath that I take, or scratching my head or any move I make. I can walk and talk, eat and sleep, I can pee and poop and many other wonders follow suit. I am asking myself where are all these thoughts coming from and where are they intended to be. It seems as though there is an invisible energy of thoughts that continue to buzz around in me.

I am in wonderment as to how my mind can learn and remember anything. Do you ever wonder how one can accomplish   a trip of out and about among the mist? How do we get there from here? How do we know that we are planning anything anywhere? How do we know when we are hungry or in need? How do we know when and who to feed. How do we just let go of stuff? How do we know if the lunatic in the grass is our friend or just a puff?   Sometimes the answers, we will just never know. I guess we should just let go and the Spirit run the show.

Tonight, I'm having thoughts of a few frog men who have been in my head. As I fantasize, the lunatic in the grass is coming to light. Like in the book of "The Shades of Gray," all I can say is Hey. Who needs all that crazy sex life anyway? I have had the shades of green and yellow, and blue and red,   now what can I say they are all gone, gone far away, like dead. - The first was a stud, the second a dud. Then the third whatever, now I'm not sure, possibly never.   In the spring of my life when I was young, I fell in love with that sweet little stud.   As the light of green turned yellow one day we each went off to follow our own way. Then along came the lunatic dressed in red, it told me to marry the dud instead. When red turned to blue, I thought I was through, being forced in divorce, depressed and in pain, I was dumped by the red frog dud man for his own gain. I am now thankful though, you see, from the dud , I was blessed with two beautiful daughters, a grandbaby and now I can be just me. Sometimes one has to pass through the fire, to reach the place where standards are higher. Words to remember, Romans 8:28 I will savor the ember.

Fifty years have passed by now. The little stud returned for a while. He picked me up to let me down. I think that now I am done with men. I am resigned to the fact that I can't go back! I will appreciate my new found Mr. Psyc man friend, but I'll just leave it at that. Like in a quote from the movie "Splendor in the Grass" - nothing can bring back the hour of splendor in the grass.

With pen in hand, I'm writing my story. My thoughts are a little abnormal and for that I am sorry. Life can be short, but I have hit 69. Memories and fantasies are all that is left from behind. The thoughts in my head turn to movements circling around and around rolling through the convoluted bends in my mind. It is amazing how the energy flows and I can exist and create life as we know.

My granddaughter, Anna spent the day with me today. She is all grown up now, what can I say. She is beautiful and talented, wise and true, wanting to manage her own life too. My only granddaughter, fifty years younger, reminds me that now I am senile and ½ century older. I want to stay young and experience the fun of what this interrupted grandma has never done, Perhaps I should smoke a weed, or lay in the grass, as the lunatic will tell me just let some time pass. Ten years can go by, and one may find life is short so it's time to move on.

It is cold out this morning. There is frost on the grass. I'll bet the lunatic is freezing its ass. "Come on inside," I said, "There is plenty of room inside my head." I've been taught to love and get along. I should know what is right or wrong. Thoughts are flowing through my mind, that it is not right to leave my family behind. My prayer for them is happiness, love and health, and almost everything else. I love my girls, granddaughter, and all, - dogs, and cat, the man, and boys, they are friendly frogs.

By now, I suppose that you notice when I write, I often like to rhyme the words just right. It is as though I have a story to tell, but along with that, there seems to be music rhythm in my head. Perhaps someday I could write a song. Dreaming in my mind leads me to find where I am strong. Thoughts rolling around and through my brain, they seem to create something for me to do. After all, I am 69, retirement is currently entering my mind. What will I do, when old age sets in? The Spirit, the lunatic, the hamster and the frogs will have to agree in the end.

How is this for the start of a song? - "I had a dream the other night, we fell in love, it was on first sight, you held me tight. We traveled on this road called life, it was fine. Then 6 kids later a beautiful wife, something happened, were now 35. I don't know why I was let go, that's life. The hurt the pain what did we gain, the kids were torn, now were worn. He moves on to another home and anothr wife, that's life. The years pass by we are now 55 work is all we know. The kids don't care, they are out there somewhere, it is all so unfair this road called life. Now at 69, as I look behind. I can't turn back, what is done is done. ,What seems so unfair could turn into air, just trying to live a love affair. At age 82, one can think they're through, at 92 who cares who is who.

The good Spirit is on the battlefield in my mind today and winning the fight just right. I am reminding myself that everyone we meet is facing a battle in their own mind that we know nothing about. We must be kind to one another. Pick up the pieces and move on. Second chances, third, fourth and even whatever it takes, turn the other cheek, give compassion to the meek. Life as we know it here, doesn't last forever. Like Dolly Pardon says in, her song – "We Had Better Get to Living While We Can." Remember we only have 100 years to live in this fleshy condition we're in.

Fall is in the air. The trees have shed their pretty leaves everywhere. Halloween has come and gone. It is time for me to shed my costume of thoughts just as the trees shed their leaves, letting go for another season. Hibernation, here I come as I enter into my mind in fantasy land. I am listening to country music and I am feeling sad. I am thinking about that special, little awesome stud man   passing through my heart. Crystal Gayle's songs are playing through my mind - " *I'll get over you ,*" and *"I'll do it All Over Again."- some of her words that I relate to are, "Was I right, Was I wrong, - A little weak, a little strong, Was it him or was it me - Oh I guess I'll never know- But I know that my heart will mend, and I know that I will smile again. - I'll get back on my feet, and then I'll do it all over again."* What a beautiful, encouraging song.

Well another day has come and gone. I am just thinking about what makes a person respond to situations the way we all do. I'm thinking about the little demented lady, who is on hospice care and who knows when, she is about to meet her maker. A son calls via phone and says, "It's ok to let go mom, we'll be ok. " I feel a little touched with interaction this way. So I take our pet therapy doggie, in for her. I say "Charlie loves you, see" She smiles, and says, "Bye, I'm going away?"   After trying to give compassionate care, her words to me are, "You're an ugly grizzly bear, stick it up your ass, you don't care.

"What's the use," my thoughts are telling me again .I'll just send this issue to the dump bucket and forgive, I'm free. Free to react the way I want to be. Is it her or is it me? Dementia it's hard to see. We all seem to have our own ideas and ways of handling   life. We all have our own issues to face. We all tend to think that our way is the best. Then issues seem to develop into stress. I want to manage things my way, so why is it so hard to just say, hey, go away.

Well, I did escape from the loony bin again, another road trip looking for another mend. I asked Doreen to accompany me. I stopped in Chattyville to pick her up . We began our trip with a booster up. Would you believe we indulged in a drink of unusual sort? She had a beer with kinky something and I had a sex on the beach with a twist. After that off we rode into the yonder to the destination we were headed for. Immediately after checking into the hotel we dipped the whirlpool there and t left for more. Then off to a fish fry we went, looking for the hot spots and froggy events. But we were so stuffed from the fish that we ate, that we were unable to participate. The next day, we journeyed up to a house on the top of a rock. There our brains became overloaded, with what we saw. We drove around the curves and bends, passing through skunk hallow and liver lane. Passing through the wooded areas our thoughts went to wondering if we were seeing Ed

Gines village. From there we travelled up on hill into a Wine Making Distill. We took the tour, tasted the wine, and were beginning to feel very fine . As we journeyed home, a heavy thunderstorm hit, we could have almost met our maker in a ditch.

I'm home now, safe and sound. It's raining turning to snow again. My little demented lady has passed away. In my mind I have to say that I am brought to the thoughts of life and death in an unexplainable way .The lunatic and frogs must be sleeping away, the Spirit is telling me, enjoy your peace and have a good day.

How can and does the mind work? I am in awe as to the mystery of my mind quirks. I can communicate in reality or I can go into my fantasy. Like a computer, I can find most anything, concerning. I can simply just live in my own little world with my own little show. I can send the unwanted messages into the dump bucket or like a computer can reboot it up.

It is November 22 today. Fifty years ago this day was on my mother's birthday. I am reminded that President Kennedy was assassinated on this day. I was 19 years old then anyway. My thoughts were clear and working fine. Memories from that day are still stored in my memory bank mind.

Thanksgiving Day has come and gone. The turkey that we ate left us all with an overloaded stomach ache. I do admit that I have a lot to be thankful for. I am thankful for this insight from a tv show. I am glad that it was not me, with this a horrible hilarious comodey. As I watched this surprising story unfold, the event took place on an emergency room floor. A lady was sitting in a toilet bowl. She was brought into the emergency room by the paramedic crew. She had proceeded to sit down for her daily chore, when un be known, someone had left the toilet seat up. and so she dropped in the hole. Her butt hit the bottom, she became stuck, and the paramedics could not get her loosened up. Her blood circulation was cut off and an emergency situation was about to take off. The doctors gathered around not knowing what to do. The maintenance men were called in too. The buzz saw man cut her off the throne. I found humor in that silly episode.

I went to see Ricky again. Perhaps I am a Jesse's girl friend. Wouldn't that be something to tell? I gave Rick a cookie once. He ate it too, right on stage in front of us, well. I wonder if possibly I am a groupie or a cougar thing. My daughter was so kind as to drive me there, we travelled through snow everywhere. His performance was solo on stage this time, he talked of all his good times left behind. I have attended many concerts that remain in my memory lane. Rick Springfield the man has made rock fame.

The lunatic has seems to have gone idle in my mind. It has been absent for quite some time. More than likely the Spirit has taken its place, cuz; God is the one that I want to embrace. I have found encouragement today. My mind has had a new beginning again, hooray!

Christmas has come and gone. My mind had wandered and events have gone on. It all started on my shopping day, I went to the dollar store, cuz I'm cheep that way. I got lots of presents to wrap anyway. Passing through my memory lane, thoughts flowed thru all the folds in my mind. The lunatic woke up and went wild that day. The Spirit went to the manger, what should I say. I remembered how as kids we used to have to make our own fun, so this is how it all begun. I wrapped the presents one by one, using old advertizing news paper, it was sort of fun. I later decided I didn't have to be so cheap, so I wrapped them again with the news paper beneath. As I counted in my mind ,the stuff multiplied, and soon I had a pile pretty high. Because I had no tree to see, I decided to string the presents around in all the rooms brilliantly. My family had to follow the trail, their presents were scattered everywhere. Somewhere along the planted line a mystery gift was soon to be found. My mind played a part in planting this gift; - a marijuana pee test was in the mix. Christmas Eve came and went. Santa missed the boat and went to another event. The thought of the Christ Child laid quietly in my head. "I am thankful for that." I said. Now on Christmas Day another surprise, the lazybones frog, Mr. Psyc man, appeared at my side. I thought perhaps he was Santa for the day, he had a beard, and what should I say. I must have been a naughty girl this year, as a gift of black lumpy coal appeared. As thoughts went back into my head about this, my ears began buzzing and my thoughts went dead. Away dasher and dancer disappeared from this scene, now I am alone again, how serene.

I am sitting in my recliner again today, I have my feet up and I am relaxed in a way. Thoughts are rolling around in my head, I am thankful that I am not yet dead. 69 years is a lot of years to live, I'm wondering by now what will have to give. My ears are buzzing and my thoughts are about to blow, the hamsters are spinning and I really do not want to let go. I'm having a brain freeze and there is pressure all around, my thoughts are muddled and I'm about to hit the ground. The lunatic is at work melting thoughts in my head. The Spirit is trying to calm me down instead. The Spirit is telling me not to worry, or fret; there will be better times to come yet. This is a day for a test of patience, I see, sooner or later my mind will embrace it.

It is NewYears Eve today. I'm watching the news on tv , and hey - what is wrong with our world this way? I heard that the mothers of new born babies can take their placentas home to eat, and this is legal, that's just plain gross, eek!   There was a baby boy raised by dogs. It has been told that he barked and walked on all four. He even ate his food off of the floor. God intervened and now he is dog boy no more. A little girl is trapped in a well, how she got there, that's sounds like hell. Two trains collided and derailed yesterday, fire balls could be seen from miles away. The Obama Care deadline today is here, now many people's insurance is about to disappear. Jobs remain difficult to find, this makes one wonder, who is left behind? There are many scandals going around today. Wieners peter is passing through the facebook news and now he is blown away. The Bengasi attack is not settled yet. Hillary is headed for the get-away jet. A Canadian Mayor is on crack cocaine .Mile Cyrus is bumping in the butt lane. The IRS is obstructing the truth. Our taxes are flying through the roof. Edward Snowman blew the whistle on our government they say. Now he is being punished in an unjust way. It is 2pm by our time today. In Dubaul Uae they are wasting 500 thousand fireworks away. Now the world is full of pot smoke and drones, this is about to knock anyone off their throne. Cigarettes are prohibited in city parks, yet marijuana can be purchased like ignorant farts. All kind off new laws are coming they say. The uighers have ties to the Taliban's, and our American soldiers are expected to leave Afghanistan . Korea has weapons of mass destruction and the Russians are headed our way. The hamsters in my head are so busy spinning away that I just need to say, " 2013 - goodbye, go away!"

Today I discovered something new to write about. The bipolar lunatic and Spirit have done a turnabout. Sitting around with my residents today, we had a discussion of how we fell into the loony bin this way. The ladies are all in their 90s ,you see, now they really have some stories to tell for you and me.   I'll write another book some day, with the title of the "The Elderly Tales." Our minds are wandering all over the place. Their life started like almost a century ago. One lady pipes up to say, "In my huge boarding house on broadway, I boarded girls and I had a popcorn stand by the way. We made lots of money selling pop corn, and the boys all flocked around. Was it the girls or the corn, who really knows, but anyway we didn't have porn." Another lady pipes up to say "I had a lot of boyfriends along the way. They all came to Rochester you see, because there were more girls than boys, 1 to 3. The boys were in their glory, they liked my big boobs, but I'm sad to say they often cheated on me too." Another said, "the bridge across the river was not yet built, we had to walk a mile just to get a hit. There were tunnels built underground, we would run and hide and could not be found. The Clinic was not yet here then, until a tornado hit, then the nuns stepped in. I remember how the city changed when IBM moved in, then more of the man ratio began."

The weather has really been cold today, 40 below wind chill they say. Possibly I may have frozen my brain. I noticed that I have acquired some new residents along the way. It seems as though some little hamsters have entered in, spinning around and around in my convoluted brain. . My daughter says that they have been there all along, she claims the hamsters to be "adhd deficits" and she is never wrong. I do tend to jump from thought to thought, just like the frogs, I jump all about. Many ideas come to me, I say, I should   patent them and you will see that I have lots of stuff inside of me. I have imagination, and fantasy, I can create thoughts that are just funny. From jumping frogs to   silly blogs, my thoughts roll around like old tree logs. My head gets heavy, and the pressure builds,   then all this movement flows into a still. My ears begin the buzzing sound then from all the commotion come   the tea pot sound.

Anxiety is bothering me today. The Spirit is attempting to chase it away. I'm sure it is the lunatic again at play, and now the hamsters have entered in and they keep spinning away. My mind is in such an unstable state, within   the convoluted bends and worm like folds there are so many avenues and holes.   This makes me wonder who is really in control. The Spirit says," I AM, just offer it up, and let it go." The lunatic says "No."   The frogs are jumping, the hamsters spinning; I am beginning to wonder am I still living? Worry will get me no where this I know. I need to just let it all go. Off to the dump bucket with this drama show.

It is snowing and blowing again outside. I am sitting in my recliner with my feet up high. I am at peace at the moment, even though I have concerns and worries. My little one in a million, angel, sweet heart, and wander-woman was sent to the ER. The ambulance came and took her away. She was having pain that wouldn't go away. Another resident, for a while has been gone, she broke her kneecap so the, nursing home rehab has been her home. The other three, are still with me, they're in their nineties, and well dementia is, what we see. My children have their issues too, they are having overwhelming stress and I don't know what to do.   I seem to be unable to help with their mess. I ask myself, "why is it that I can help the others, yet my own family has to settle for less?"   The Spirit says, "I AM here, no need to fear, things will work out and the issues will disappear." The lunatic seems to have disappeared, the frogs have jumped away, and the hamsters, well they're still here spinning in the rear.

I am watching the cancer telethon today. I too have been diagnosed with cancer, but it has gone away. Remission they say, so don't feel sorry for me, I'll be ok. Because of this thought, I am reminded of circles today. We all have them, circles, circles of people and things gathered along the way. You see we are all traveling on our own path in this life, and in our own mind we keep circling in time. We seem to be searching for something, perhaps a new find. Thoughts are telling me that we are all here for a reason and we all will have our own season.

The hamsters are really spinning around in my head today, as I am sitting here in my chair watching the Joyce Meyers Enjoying Everyday show. I am quite irritated and short with compassion at the moment. I am sleep deprived from being interrupted and night time awoken. Several times last night the little one in a million wander woman roamed around. Redirection brought naughty words and thoughts to sort out. I tried to find some peace in this loony bin box. I found myself headed for the pity me room in my disturbed brain celled mind. The hope and change Obama has touched us with has his dictator attitude causing a bind. The mind healing frog man, Mr Psyc, has moved away. My befuddled mind is in the state of disarray. I am really uptight today. I am bearing ill feelings with my life this way. The Spirit speaks up to say, "Attitude can make a difference, happiness is something one decides, and worry will be useless." I am questioning myself at this time, "how can I possibly be happy with all these issues stuck in my mind?" As I reflect on my life and my happiness today , I just want to live my life in the right way. I am aware of how restless I have become. I have decided that I am going rearrange my mind set and look for some fun.

Thinking about where I am at my age of 69, my first thought is not to let my children fall behind. I cannot do this on my own. I have come to the realization that God is the one in control. His Spirit is inside of me this I know. Now with my actions, I must show the way to follow and how to let go. At 69, I can be upright or I can be down, passing through this convoluted cell filled mind. As the thoughts start spinning away, the lunatic shows up, and the hamsters are at play. The frogs are jumping and are upside down. This befuddled mind is mixed in a puddle of lost and it needs to be found.

I'm back into the mood of listening to music again. I am in my memory lane of thoughts trying sooth my soul. I am listening to the songs by Sylvia, - *"Heart on the Mend"* - *"Love signs are flashing, I've come a*

long way, I've danced with a lot of cowboys along the way."
And then there is *"Sweet Yesterday "and , "Snapshot" –*
"the one he didn't know I got."

My memories of relationships with men have just not been good. The lunatic must be at play and the hamsters are spinning away. Most of the frogs have jumped away. I don't understand why, but I have to say, I did have a lot of love that I could have given away. The lunatic is telling me, "Jesus was a man." I am asking myself "why then have I had a such difficult time." Somewhere in my brain there must be a discernment rail to set this thought free on this convoluted trail. I am unable to let go of these thoughts today, I'll just listen to more music in my own way.

Its 5am, my mind is on alert. The hamsters have been spinning away on my dreamland road. I had just woke up from an unusual foggy type dream. Thoughts were really jumping into my memory lane stream. I was sitting on a stool behind the window of a drive up taco joint. There was a pile of pictures that a frog man was printing out. As he was multitasking, and passing free tacos out, I was watching in wonderment of what this was all about. He said, "Don't you know, we need to show some kindness, there is a world crisis today. Jobs are hard to find, don't leave them behind. Mind your own business, and get out of mine." His boss came along and determined that he was doing wrong. Then I was directed get along. The lunatic inside of me was saying this is not the time for charity ,so I left the scene to head for my car. Then out of nowhere, came a flying star. As I put the pictures into my car, I felt a pain protrude through my heart. The lunatic then appeared and, said "now get in the pit." The Spirit came along and picked me out, I was placed on a bench by the taco joint. As I looked up towards the sky I saw that another object headed out. It came closer and closer, bigger and bigger, and to my surprise it was a flicking ticker. I thought this was the end of me. However to my surprise the object disapated in the breeze. .When I became inquisitive about the meaning of this, a little frog man appeared out of the mist. He was announcing   a new kind of invention and was experimenting within a new dimension. He just lost control of his destination, and was forced to land in my premonition. In my mind, I will just place this in my fantasy because I just don't know what to make of this. I then woke up from this confusion of thoughts, the lunatic, the hamsters, and the frogs; they were all really busy jumping about.

My daughter took me to a street beat concert last night. This was really what it was about. Hip hop acrobats were jumping around, and garbage can drummers making awesome sounds.   It was hard to believe that the rhythm they made created the desire for the other entertainers to spin around on their heads. This brings to my attention, the unique gifts that we all have, we each have been blessed in different ways. To roll around on one's head is not for me, but to enjoy the talents of this kind is really something to see.

It is snowing out again, the wind is blowing. It's 20 below, with 59 below wind-chill. - freezing cold. My fingers are frozen, and well my nose, I don't know. My brain has entered into remote control. I have to warm it somehow so I can think. The snowplows are out and making noise. They have plowed seven foot high piles of snow and plugged me in my house so there is nowhere to go. Its blizzard conditions embracing the scene, advisories are out, and there's no way to move about. Now is the time to go into my fantasy,   I'll just imagine myself on a cruise ship, riding high on the waves in the western seas.

It is 1:10 am. Little one in a million wander woman is up wandering again. It is unexplainable how a personality can change from being a little angel to a pesky little thing. Sundowners, I guess is the answer for this. The other night she was up seven times, teasing the lunatic in my mind. The Spirit was telling me to curb my temper. She can't help her confused behavior. I should really try to understand that brain changes have entered her mind. In reality we are all subject to the unknown of what we might become if karma should turn around. There is no need for anxiety. I am far from perfect, and there are many errors of my way. All I can say is that I can't even help myself so I must learn to obey. I'll offer this up, and cast it away.

I have to tell one on myself today. Yesterday I helped my daughter move some of her belongings away. I set my glasses on a kitchen stand only for them to fall down. Little did I know that when they dropped on the floor, a lens fell out and remained there? I proceeded to wear my glasses for the rest of the day, that way. Now I ask myself, how could I not know that the lens was missing." After I got home from working all day, I removed the glasses , and I have to say , I found one lens was gone . Now the lunatic in my mind woke up to say," you goofy old lady, your 69, your losing your noodles in your mind, you won't last long. The frogs woke and started jumping about, not knowing which end was up. The hamsters started spinning around and around, 69 looked the same whether up or down. Panic and anxiety started hitting my brain, "what if, my mind goes funny and I become loony before my golden year time?" The good Spirit spoke the words this way, "my child, laugh at yourself, you had a good day, this too will pass away". Now we are not supposed to worry and fret, I can still see and I am thankful for that. My mind could be going through some changes in life, but I am not dead yet and I am still 69. I'll run these thoughts through my convoluted brain , I'll laugh at myself and I'll say " what difference does it make anyway ." I am already in this loony box, I am no different than the others, only age in time, they are 96, and I am 69. One resident's pipes up to say " I can't see," another says " my hearing is gone." Another says " look at me, I can't even walk". Now the hamsters in my mind keep spinning around, life goes on and we begin again.

It is 5am Sunday morning. I am awakened by the noise of a resident moving around. She is up dressing getting ready to for church that is not until 9.

I can't sleep, so I am reading on my computer about a story of "The Wrong Funeral." The daughter of Mary was sitting alone on a hard pew, lonely and grieving the loss of her mother dear. The other family members all had someone to comfort them in their sorrow. Her mother had been her best friend. Now her mother was gone, she was all alone, and broken hearted.   Shortly before the sermon took place, a man appeared and took a space next to the daughter. He whispered to her, "Sorry I'm late." Then he asked, "why are they saying her name is Mary, when her name it is Margret, she is my mother." "No, this is my mother, Mary," the grief stricken daughter replied. Then they whispered and discovered, they giggled and drew laughter together. The man was at the wrong funeral. After the service was over, they met outside in the parking lot, they set a date to meet again, and because of that scene, their love affair began. Today they are married and the daughter is lonely no more. Did God send the man to her to open a new door?

I am back with thoughts rolling through head. My good Spirit is reminding me of issues and episodes that have entered in there. The words that are flowing through the cells in my mind are bringing music memories from way back time. I am reminded that God is close to the broken hearted and all things are possible with God when we work together. When we trust and obey, He will show us the way.

Music is so soothing to my soul. As I was thinking of the man at the wrong funeral, thoughts of my mother come back to my head. She was my best friend and now she is gone but yet, she has been here all along. I never had a grandma, so my mother was the grand – ma to me. And now I am thinking of her through this song " Holes in the walls of Heaven," by Steve Warner - " *How I cried when the sky let go with the cold and lonesome rain, Momma smiled and said , don't be sad child, Grandma's watching you today, cuz there's holes in the floor of heaven and her tears are pouring down, that's how you know she is watching, wishing she could be here now , and sometimes if you're lonely just remember she can see, cuz there's holes in the floor of heaven and she is watching you and me.*" In my mind I know that if my mother could be here now, she would be here comforting you and me. I can vividly remember my mother's funeral. I was sitting on a hard pew also, in the funeral home with no arms around me. My family all had their spouses and I was alone you see. My girls were there somewhere and they had their own grief to bear. They were sad a morning too, Grandma was gone from everywhere. I was unable them help them with relief from their grief, cuz I was so alone myself.

My daughter Sue is a radio DJ, and she requested of me, to listen to the radio as we passed through the country to the cemetery.   The procession of Grandmas body from the funeral home to the burial ground was 13 minutes long. On the radio,   I heard Sue dedicate this song for Grandma for her final way home. - *"Free Bird"* by Leonard Skinner,*" - "If I leave here tomorrow would you still remember me, for I must be traveling on now, cuz there are so many places I've got to see, -but if I stay here with you girl things just couldn't be the same, cuz I am as free as a bird now and this bird cannot change."* - The total lyrics from this song was13 minutes long, lasting through the whole country side procession. Grandma is gone.

The lunatic has gone into hibernation, and the frogs are sleeping in the creek, the hamsters have stopped spinning and the Spirit has been dwelling in my sleep. I have experienced answered prayers. I have seen with my own eyes how God works through people in disguise. I am broken hearted and lonely now. I have had many new beginnings and I have shut down. I need to be needed, I am in that role now. I can see that God has placed me here somehow. My prayer is that I can complete this call. I feel now, as though I have done it all. I have done a full circle and have gone around another bend from 15 to 69, does this cycle ever end?

It is 5am in the morning. I have been interrupted again. I was engaged in a dream with the voices in my head when the wander woman woke me instead. I got up to direct her back to bed. "Kiss me ass," she said. The lunatic was awake and at play, the frogs were jumping and the hamster were spinning away. I thought, "Is this how I am going to begin my day?" The Spirit piped up to say, "My child you will be ok, just let these thoughts flow away."

I am again planning a trip to get away. I'm going to Phoenix, I m going to fly away. My friend Taren is going to accompany me. The thoughts of the Phoenix bird are entering me. I am asking myself now, what will I find.

The legend of the phoenix bird has a meaning, you see. It is about a bird that refused to die. From the ashes to resurrection and rebirth, the mythical bird will again rise. My lunatic thoughts have carried me down a negative slide, - our airline tickets have stressed our lives. The terrorists are stuffing explosives in tooth paste tubes, and sending lasers in the air, messing with airplanes everywhere. There is snow on the ground here, that s 'scary too. The good Spirit says, "can't you see, look on the positive side like the phoenix bird you can fly away too. It is by the grace of God and it is a honorable gift to be chosen to serve in this caregiving mist. However a short get away will save the way from burnout and like the phoenix bird, renewal and restart will begin new day .

I have just returned home from a Jim Brinkman concert that my daughter took me to. Jim Brinkman is the most awesome, talented and gifted pianist , that's for sure. His gifted fingers playing the piano keys create a sensuous feeling inside my head. Among some of his music with the lyrics he wrote, are in his words ," *My Valentine ,*" - "*if there were no words, no way to speak, I would still hear you, if there were no tears no way to feel inside, I'd still feel for you. *" Other awesome songs are rolling through like the *"Rainbow Sky,"* - *"It's a Beautiful World "* and *" The Love of my Life. "*

It is Sunday morning, 10:30 am. The hamsters have awakened and are spinning again. There is the buzzing in my ears that does not seem to disappear. It is as though the buzzing is not in my head, but coming from the environment out there somewhere. I am sitting in my recliner chair, with my feet up and my uncombed hair. The residents are sleeping and I don't seem to care. It has snowed outside again. Another four inch pile has hit the shovels end. I'm thinking about my upcoming trip to Phoenix. Am I being selfish? This snowy terrain and loony bin has tired me out and I need to begin again. I was awakened seven times last night. Little wander woman was up roaming around and seemed to want a verbal fight. Another resident was telling me she was cold and could not breathe, and another just had to get up to pee. Then more noise began at the break of dawn, another was dressing for church which was not until nine. My interrupted kitty had wanted to lay by me, but now that I am awake she is no where around that I can see. Poor me, the hamsters have awakened the lunatic, and now they are at play. It is now 11am, time for me to get busy and make plans for my getaway. The Spirit has stepped in to say, "Don't you know, it is time to make lunch and do your daily chores".

Well, the time has come and gone. The Phoenix bird has crossed my mind. My friend and I traveled to Phoenix. Like the mythology stories of the

Phoenix bird, I have a lot stored in my head now and it is about another rebirth. It is no secret how people and places are meant to be, and here are some adventures that have entered into me. Our flight was delayed 2 days due to blizzard conditions. We were late in arriving to our destination. We were on our way to a Joyce Meyers Conference. More spiritual awakenings headed for my conscience. Arriving late we had no prepared plans, but we went to the conference, hoping to enter in. The audience was large and the venue room small, but we did manage to see the nights call. After the conference we waited for a no show ride, only to be placed to rescue another standing by. It was midnight before we finally got home. Home was at the Sheraton, a fancy hotel. Many of our hours were spent by the pool side there. With the sun shining down, I got wonderful and suntan. I had a lot of time for thoughts of reflection. The Spirit was present leading me in the right direction. I have so much to be thankful for. -My family, my friends, my health, my wealth, my mind. It was good to let the past fall behind. Like the Phoenix bird, renewal was the find. Rest and relaxation was interrupted as my thoughts kept spinning around. Why I was so lucky to make this trip and the others were stuck in the loony bin pit. God was good to me wanting me to rest. I was experiencing conditions of the best. The Lunatic tried to enter in, making me to feel guilty for going. I had responsibility to the ladies at home, and one was on her way out, with her maker knocking at her door. To expect my children to cover for me was spinning the hamsters. My worry for my granddaughter with her struggles of today, breaks my heart, it is hope I pray. They all did fine and I got away, I went walking, swimming, golfing, and drinking every day. I no longer feel as though my home is a loony bin, I am homesick for my family and my friends. I know home where I belong.

Leaving the sunshine, and peaceful environment, led me back home to the snow blizzard 5 foot high snow drift covered environment. Arriving home, the residents were a little sick with the cold and flu in the mist. One of the residents was in the process of her journeys end . This sends thoughts rolling through my mind, - life is short. We all must try to understand the others pain, help when you can and be kind. Forgive, forget, birth a renewal every day, find a phoenix in your life and move on that way.

The dear resident passed away yesterday. She received her wings and is on her way. I am feeling emotional now. Life is short, what else can I say. The song, "You only have 100 years to live," by the band Five for Fighting, is playing though my mind, as I listen to this song, many memories of people are entering in. Many residents have come and gone, some have passed away, and some are so alone. Some of my friends have passed away too, memories of them have left me feeling blue.

I am dedicating this song to my granddaughter Anna. Anna is 19 today, but to me I still vision her younger like 15 because it is hard for me to let go. She is a young woman on her own way. Some of the lyrics and music from this song " *100 Years*" by Five for Fighting, are playing over and over in my head. Some of the words of this song are here instead. - *"I'm 15 years for a moment, counting the ways to where you are,   there's still time for you, there is a wish better than this, when you only got a hundred years to live".* I am thinking of how Anna helped me yesterday as another sweet lady passed away. Time is short. We must not waste our time away . "Be happy," the Spirit would say. I once started a song to share with Anna, it went this way. - *"It's a good day for loving Gods way; it's a good day for saying just hey."* I never finished this, I'll leave that for Anna.

The voices in my head have been quiet today. The lunatic must have gone astray. The frogs have jumped away, and the hamsters are spinning in their in their own world of play. The Spirit seems busy trying to comfort me. It is telling me life continues on eternally. I'll rest a little and prepare for a new day, I'll be ok.

Well today is the "ides of March." I am wondering what is this about? I know it is the middle, the half way mark of March, and in ancient Roman times, it was the day Julius Cesar went out. This day, is suppose to send out some evil vibes, like "beware of the ides of March." My hamsters are spinning with discernment today.

My spirit is sending this song rolling through my mind, "Be not Afraid" - I go before you always, come follow me, and I will give you rest." The lunatic is hanging out in my dump bucket, and the frogs are jumping with joy.

Spring is around the corner, and the snow is melting away. I am missing the latest resident that just passed away. She was another resident dear to me. I am wondering where she is now and will she recognize the other angels in Gods family. I'll just pass through this thought now because my life is winding down, I am still 69. Have I missed something in this life I wonder , or is there another season to come?

The ides of the March scenario has hit me again. The lunatic is at big time play. My mind is about to be blown away. Damn ole Obama and Income tax! I have worked very hard all year long, and have made less money than the years past. Now, when my income is low, why do I have to pay more? I say, "You know, if Obama don't get us with his unaffordable health care act, he'll screw over us with our income tax. Do you think he cares about this?" My hamster is spinning away. The frogs are jumping with play. The lunatic in my mind says go smoke a weed. Laying all jokes aside I had a dream about this. The other night I dreamt that I did smoke a weed. It was given to me. The weed consisted of two sausage links rolled up in a paper towel. I thought I can't smoke all of this, so I discarded one for a while. When I proceeded to smoke the remains, I got a little weird. When I woke from my dream and began to think, what was this all about, is my mind is about to shrink?

April 1st is around the bend. I wonder what is in store for me then. Today it is raining and there is still snow on the ground. The thoughts in my head seem to weigh ten pounds, I feel heavy, weary, and need some rest. My sleep is still interrupted nightly, little wander woman sometimes gets a little flighty. She is a sweetheart in the day time, I love her dearly, but oh my gosh my nights get weary. The hamsters keep rolling around and around, the ADHD notion makes me act like a clown. I am not perfect, you know, and I see, these thoughts are just thoughts coming from my olfactory.

This morning I awoke from another dream. As usual it was a bit extreme. I dreamt that I was sitting by a pool side in Hawaii, and that I was eating bamboo shoots, pineapple nuts and drinking a bacardi. Then I turned around to look in a mirror and there was a bunch of grapes growing out of my ear. Horror over took me as I woke up. The lunatic was on the scene and was laughing at me. April fool's day it is, I see.

Its 3 am another day again .I can't sleep because I've been dreaming. I woke up and forgot the dream but the words with this music kept radiating in me .The words from the song " *"Here I am Lord," by Dan Schulte,* goes like this, *" I the Lord of sea and sky, I have heard your people cry, all who dwell in dark and sin, my hand will save – I who made the stars at night ,I will make their darkness bright, who will bear my light to them, whom shall I send?- Here I am Lord , is it I Lord, I have heard you calling in the night- I will go Lord, if you lead me, I will hold your people in my heart. "* After this awesome awakening my hearts' vibration is over flowing. In my mind the lunatic, frogs and hamsters are on the run and the Spirit keeps singing on. Today is going to be a very good day.

I am sitting in my chair again here today, with my feet up and, and I am coughing with a cold virus that won't go away. On the tv , they're talking about a lunar eclipse that is happening tonight. Something is about to drastically change. It is about the moon turning red, a divine sight, amen. The earth gets between the sun and the moon and casts upon the moon a red shadow . They call this a blood moon, and that God it is trying to communicate with us in a supernatural way. The book of Genesis says that God uses the sun and the moon and the stars for signs. There seems to be a sense of that now in our world time. Something is about to change. Today is Passover, with Easter coming on? We should take heed and listen to what this means.

My bipolar mind is having thoughts of doom and gloom. The lunatic is wild and having fun in my head. It is encouraging me to believe that a drastic change is ahead. There is so much chaos in our world today. There's talk of a new world order. Currency as we know it, we will have no more. Don't work, Obama says, let the government dictate. Were on the road to bondage, and I know that I will hate it. There are shootings and stabbings and fires too. There are bomb threats, a missing air jet, and no one knows who is who. My hamsters keep spinning away, and the frogs, all they know is how to play. My spirit says " breathe, tomorrow will bring a new day."

It is April 16th today. I am sitting in my chair, listening to piano music played by my most recent resident here. She is 94. The music is beautiful and is entering my ear. She tells me that she has not had a lesson in her life time,she does not read notes, and plays the music all by ear. "This is truly a gift," I say. In my mind, this music seems to have put the lunatic to sleep, the hamsters in a rhythm, the frogs relaxing. The good Spirit is spreading peace and comfort through the house. I am reminded with my own thoughts, that this is Gods way of sending us His promise of comfort and rest. Her piano music that is now playing *"Somewhere over the Rainbow."* I am very much enjoying.

It's still snowing away. I woke up from a dream that someone was digging a hole beside my house. A huge round boulder came rolling out down a hill to across the street. The house that the bolder hit caught fire so I called 911.When they asked for the address I began apologizing because I realized that this was a dream. I then thought that maybe they should come out anyway when I noticed someone was burying a little red car . I discovered that it was my neighbor and we got into a verbal war. I told him he should bury his garbage in his own dump because he had a bigger yard.

Today on the news there was talk of how the buffalo were on the run. Yep, and other animals were leaving Yellowstone in record groves. Do the animals know something that we do not know? The seismic activity is up and there is speculation that volcanoes are imminent to erupt. Just recently there has been earthquake activity in

LA and mudslides in Washington, and more snow coming our way. Our country and Israel are being threatened by terrorists . Another shooter at Fort Hood killed 3 fellow service men and injured many more before blowing himself away. Could it be possible that our Maker is getting fed up with our activities of living in all this sinful stuff?

I think an Angel passed by my house today. My Spirit said sometimes things happen that way. The lunatic must have been at play teasing me with stress . There was a fire smoldering outside my house in the surrounding foundation mulch. I was sick and wasted away, when a loud rapid knocking came banging on the door . A gentleman said, "there is a fire outside your house, do you have some water, I'll put it out." To my surprise it was melting the siding, a dangerous fire was arising. But the Good Samaritan intervened and stopped this cycle right away. We were spared from a disaster, and for that I am thankful, I say.

It was May 3rd,7pm. The sun was going down and there was a pink and red banded rainbow across the sky. I could not tell if I was north or south, but there were hundreds of windmills turning about. I was sitting in my little Jimmy all alone and in frenzy. I had time to think about stuff. I was lost and out of gas. The lunatic was at play, teasing me with, "how did you get here from there?" My hamsters were spinning, and the frogs jumping, the good Spirit said, " calm down," you will be found and forgiven." Luckily I had a cell phone along, I call my daughter Sara, " I don't know when I will be home." We had such a fun day, me and my friend. We had traveled a long the Mississippi Riverway . We called it our road trip sailing for garbage. We followed the garage sale signs as we gathered and loaded. Along the way we came upon two beautiful little kittens, free, and cute we just had to take them. Alveria and Alvin Winer we named them and in a little cage we took them. Alveria was a cute little black girl kitty and Alvin, her brother was gray with tiger spot twirls. So Doreen adopted Alveria, and I, well , my mind had a change .I realized that my kitty at home might not like this game. So on our way home we passed by a humane place , little Alvin was welcomed into the kitty orphanage. Now my hamsters kept spinning, putting guilt on my mind of how did I get mixed up into this heartbreaking find. To separate the kittys was not kind. I had time to think about this when I was lost . So the sos distress sign went out, my daughter Sue googled my whereabouts. My son in law Shaun set out to rescue me, "the package" (me) was picked up. Yipee!

I heard on the news today, a way to stay young , and have a good healthy mind, preventing alzheimers dementia and all preserving stuff is that young blood is the answer. Not only can the young generation hand their future over , but donating their blood is the answer. The old folks can continue living and the young ones can keep on giving. Now what is the world coming to? It is true that life is in blood, but this is really a weird thought - eweee – dump bucket here it comes.

Mothers day has come and gone. I was honored as though I was a queen on a throne. My girls have been so very kind to me, gifting me with roses, cake, and candy. I even received a special gift, the book,"Magnificiant Vibration," by the author, Rick . He is a famous Rock Star , and well , his book now I shouldn't tell. I am not surprised about this novel that he wrote, but his fantasies are really a bit remote. I think that he is just like me, having a lunatic inside his convoluted memory.

It is now May 10th. The humid and hot weather is holding us in suspense . Tornados are circling around and around. Some have even hit the ground. So far we have not faced the lost and found, but others unfortunately have flown off the ground.

I am closing in on the end of my writing time. Soon I will leave 69 behind. My lunatic is still sticking in my mind. It says , " I am not done picking on you. I'll find you in your 70s. room." The frogs are still jumping , I met another last night, he was singing karooke and hold me tight. My hamsters keep spinning away, my daughter says," they are a.d.d. (attention deficit) I'm sure to say." The good Spirit says , " there is no giving up, another year older is like deeper in debt.

May 20 an announcement was made. "You're a Great Grandma," my Grand baby says. "I'm having a baby it is on the way." Little eggy   will become a little bundle of joy, now 2 months in the oven, with a December due day. Life is full of suprises, and this one I have to say will enter into my "happy place." My hamsters are spinning away in joy. the frogs are jumping in celebration ,and the good Spirit is blessing .This is a new beginning, I am happy to say. God has blessed Anna in a very special way.

June 1st is around the corner, the 15th will soon be here. My mind is settling down some, my thoughts in the convolutions of my brain mass are clear. I am reminiscing memories of what I hold dear. In my heart I am thankful for the God that has given me life. I am thankful for Jesus and that we can begin again. I am thankful for our children, because family is what it is about. My prayer is for their health and happiness and that our circle of life continues on . The blessings that God has given us the gift Life.

I'm ending 69 tonight, I am now pushing 70. Pinacolattas and cinnamon tea are entering the brain cells inside of me. I am swirling and twirling and enjoying my life. I am free to believe and I am free to love. I can enjoy my fantasy however I want. I am free to be me just as you see. Who care who is who and what is in store for me or you. 10 years can pass by then I'll be almost 82.

Music is flowing through my mind tonight. It is playing over and over as I am winding down. The lunatic has slipped away and is lost in the grass. The frogs are in a puddle and the hamsters are at rest. My Spirit has begun singing this song . It is "The Story of my Life," by One Direction. This is the description of the trophy for my time, it is mine " in the mind 69."

In this song "The Story of My Life," the lyricist, One Direction, describes the stories written in the walls, the stories written in his heart and that when he goes home the words will be written in stone. But he will be gone, and like him, I will be gone too. I also wish for my story to stay written in stone. I want to be remembered when I'm on my way home, and I don't want my story to be gone. – I've been waiting for this time to come around. Running after life is like, chasing the clouds. This story of my life, I'll take it home. I'll drive all night, I'll keep it warm – I'm 70 now on my way home.